B Evans
onatelli, Jen Jones,
hris Evans /
27.99

EDGE
BOOKS™

HOLLYWOOD
ACTION HEROES

CHRIS
EVANS

BY JEN JONES

CAPSTONE PRESS
a capstone imprint

Edge Books are published by Capstone Press,
1710 Roe Crest Drive, North Mankato, Minnesota 56003
www.mycapstone.com

Library of Congress Cataloging-in-Publication Data
Names: Jones, Jen, author.
Title: Chris Evans / by Jen Jones.
Description: North Mankato, Minnesota : Capstone Press, 2016. | Series: Edge
  books: Hollywood action heroes | Includes bibliographical references and
  index.
Identifiers: LCCN 2016004949| ISBN 9781515712381 (library binding : alk.
  paper) | ISBN 9781515712985 (ebook pdf)
Subjects: LCSH: Evans, Chris, 1981—Juvenile literature. | Actors—United
  States—Biography—Juvenile literature.
Classification: LCC PN2287.E77 D66 2016 | DDC 791.4302/8092—dc23
LC record available at http://lccn.loc.gov/2016004949

Editorial Credits
Linda Staniford, editor; Kyle Grenz, designer;
Eric Gohl, media researcher; Gene Bentdahl, production specialist

Photo Credits
Alamy: AF Archive, 4–5, 12–13, 19, 21, Pictorial Press Ltd, 22–23; AP Photo:
Invision/Colin Young-Wolff, 27; Newscom: Album/20th Century Fox, 17, Album/
Curran, Douglas/Paramount Pictures, 15, PacificCoastNews, 8, WENN Photos/
BT1, 9; Shutterstock: Everett Collection, 7 (top), Galiptynutz, 7 (bottom), Jaguar
PS, 25, 29, Lauren Orr, 11, s_bukley, cover, 1

Design Elements: Shutterstock

Printed in China.
042016   007737

TABLE OF CONTENTS

Chapter 1

Hero Style

Ever since Chris Evans won the heroic role of Captain America, his career has gotten a shot of super-soldier serum. To date, his movies have made more than $5 billion at the box office. Chris's movie star looks, dry humor, and Boston charm have won him fans all over the world.

Chris goes all-out to play his role as Captain America. He spends a great deal of time preparing physically and mentally for every new project. Chris also enjoys doing his own stunts whenever possible, just like a true action hero!

Chris as Captain America in *Captain America: The First Avenger*

But what lies behind this on-screen crusader's shield? Chris is deeply devoted to his family and Boston roots. He stays down-to-earth, never losing sight of those who helped him rise to greatness. There are many sides to this talented actor, just like the superheroes he brings to life.

A Hero is Born

Ever hear the phrase "Boston Strong?" Most Bostoners have a great amount of hometown pride. Chris Evans is no exception.

Born on June 13, 1981, Chris spent his childhood in Boston. His family later moved to nearby Sudbury when he was 11 years old. Like many people in Massachusetts, Chris was raised Catholic in an Irish-Italian family. He attended Lincoln-Sudbury High School. During this time he acted in school plays and Concord Youth Theatre, Massachusetts productions.

Now that he's a major Hollywood star, Chris lives part of the time in Los Angeles. However, he still strives to spend at least five months per year in his favorite place—Boston. "Boston will always be home," he has said.

Fast Fact

Chris hasn't forgotten where he comes from. In 2014 he and his agent donated a brand-new 83-seat **black box theater** to the Concord Youth Theatre.

Whenever he is not making movies, Chris likes to go back home to Boston to spend time with his family.

black box theater—a simple theater, usually with black walls, that can be adapted to any kind of performance

It's in the Blood

Chris' love of drama definitely runs in the family. Long before he lit up the big screen, he hit the stage at Concord Youth Theatre. His mother, Lisa, has been Artistic Director there since 1998. But his older sister, Carly, first gave Chris the acting bug. She often directed family puppet shows and later studied theater at New York University.

Chris took his sisters, Carly (left) and Shanna (right), and his mother Lisa (center) to the premiere of Avengers: Age of Ultron in 2015.

Chris' brother and two sisters are very much involved with the arts. Carly has directed plays at Lincoln-Sudbury High School and summer shows at Concord Youth Theatre. Chris' younger sister Shanna is an art teacher. She often helps with Concord Youth Theatre's set design and costumes. Chris' younger brother, Scott, landed **recurring** TV roles on *One Life to Live* and *Law & Order: Criminal Intent*. Chris comes from an entire family of performers!

recurring—happening over and over again

Scott Evans (right) is two years younger than his brother Chris.

Fast Fact

Chris has several tattoos dedicated to the people he loves. One tattoo is the Japanese character for "family," which is on Chris's right arm.

Chapter 3

Taking Flight

Like many actors, Chris got his start in a casting office. However, unlike most, it wasn't by attending a casting call or audition. Instead, Chris did a summer **internship** in New York City when he was a high school junior. There he got an inside look at how auditions work and how actors are hired. When not interning, Chris took acting classes with other **aspiring** actors.

Chris originally wanted to be an artist and go to college. After that fateful summer, he went back to Boston for his senior year at Lincoln-Sudbury. Yet he still headed into the city every week for auditions. When he scored a role on a TV **pilot**, it was time to rethink his life plans. Chris' future in acting was taking shape.

internship—a temporary job in which a person works with and learns from experienced workers

aspiring—having a goal to do something specific

pilot—a test to see how a TV series performs with an audience before it is bought by a network

"When the [TV] pilot got picked up and took me to [Los Angeles], we decided, 'Maybe college can wait,'"

–Chris on his career choice

Times Square in New York is the heart of the Broadway Theater District. Working in New York changed Chris' career.

Not Just Another Teen Heartthrob

Chris has starred in several big-screen blockbuster films. But he got his start on the small screen. His first TV role was in the short-lived Fox series *Opposite Sex*. He played one of just three guys in an otherwise all-girl school. Though the series lasted only eight episodes, Chris' performance helped him land parts on *The Fugitive* and *Boston Public*.

Those small-screen roles helped set the stage for Chris' first big break: *Not Another Teen Movie*. Released in 2001, the movie poked fun at the **formulaic** teen films of the 1980s and 1990s. Chris showed off his funny side as a high school football jock.

formulaic—following a predictable pattern

"When I found out I had to take off my shirt in *Teen Movie*, I panicked and hit the gym. I was like, 'I can't be 140 pounds—I need to put on a little bit of muscle.'"

–Chris on preparing for action roles

Chris starred with Mia Kirshner, who played his sister in *Not Another Teen Movie*.

Making An Impression

After *Not Another Teen Movie*, Chris was ready to become a leading man. The year 2004 was a big one for the actor, who landed lead roles in two movies. The first was *The Perfect Score*. This comedy featured teenage characters who plan an elaborate **heist** to pass the SAT exam. The film paired Chris with future *Avengers* co-star Scarlett Johansson. It was the first of several movies they would star in together.

Next up was *Cellular*. In this thriller, Chris' character races to solve a kidnapping case using only a cell phone. Before filming began, Chris trained to do high-speed car chases at a Los Angeles stunt school.

heist—a robbery

On *Cellular*, Chris worked with successful actors like William H. Macy and Kim Basinger. He took the time to soak in their knowledge. "It was kind of like going to acting class every day."

–**Chris on working with Hollywood stars**

Chris (center) and Scarlett Johansson (right) first worked together in *The Perfect Score.*

Chapter 4

Let the Action Begin

In 2005 the film *Fantastic Four* took the legendary comic book superheroes to movie screens everywhere. The movie also transformed Chris from rising actor to superstar. He played one of the four main superheroes, alongside actors Jessica Alba, Michael Chiklis, and Ioan Gruffudd. Together their characters battled the enemy using superpowers gained during a **cosmic** storm. Chris' character, Johnny Storm, had the ability to fly. He could control fire and toss fireballs, earning him the nickname "The Human Torch." He could even set his entire body on fire with a single command: "Flame on!"

Fast Fact

Chris Evans improvised many of his lines in *Fantastic Four*.

Despite mixed reviews, the film made more than $330 million worldwide. Thanks to its success, a **sequel** was released in 2007. *Fantastic Four: Rise of the Silver Surfer* reunited the actors to save Earth from the evil Galactus. In this story the Human Torch could assume others' superpowers simply by touching them. The film's final fight scene featured Chris' character harnessing all four heroes' superpowers to take on Dr. Doom.

cosmic—having to do with the universe and the stars

improvised—made up on the spot

sequel—a story that continues an existing story, taking it forward in time

Pushing the Limits

Chris tapped into his inner daredevil yet again in 2009's *Push*. Chris' character moves things with his mind using a special power called **telekinesis**. He partners with a young psychic played by Dakota Fanning. Together they work to take down an evil organization known as The Division.

telekinesis—the ability to move something by thought or willpower, without using physical force

Unlike the Fantastic Four movies, the film relied very little on computer-generated imagery (CGI) for special effects. Instead, the stunts were done in real time. It was a huge thrill for Chris, despite getting some bumps and bruises. "It's a fun day's work when you get to go and get chucked around a room," Chris said.

One of the most intense moments in *Push* involved a "telekinetic gunfight." Chris' character controls weapons with his mind to take on two bad guys. One stunt required him to slide all the way across the room on his back while shooting a gun. "To me, it was the quintessential action movie shot," he has said. "I felt like a kid in a candy store. You want to get the pads on and dive in and get your hands dirty."

Chris plays telekinetic Nick Gant in *Push*.

The Greatest American Hero

When Chris landed the role of Captain America in 2011, it sealed his place in the Marvel Cinematic Universe. *Captain America: The First Avenger* was the first of six films in which Chris would play the superhuman Steve Rogers.

While playing Captain America, Chris has enjoyed doing many of his own stunts. In *Captain America: The Winter Soldier* (2014), he took his mask off to show just how real the action was. But sometimes things got a little too real. For one scene in that movie, Chris spent three rough days shooting in a glass elevator fighting off 12 burly stuntmen. Afterward, he was a bit the worse for wear. But Chris accepts the sore muscles and bruises as part of the job.

"The scariest stuff isn't the things you think it'd be—the jumps and explosions, all of that. It's actually the fight sequences, the hand-to-hand combat ... Going up against these other big guys and knowing you have to properly fight one another can be scary."

–Chris on doing his own stunts

Fast Fact

The Marvel movies aren't Chris' only comic-based films. He also played a skateboarder-turned-action movie star in *Scott Pilgrim vs. The World*.

In the Marvel Cinematic Universe, Chris plays Steve Rogers, who is transformed into Captain America thanks to a "Super-Soldier serum."

The "A"-Team

Chris has more than 40 acting credits to his name. However, it's surprisingly easy for him to pick his career highlight so far—*The Avengers* (2012). "It's the biggest thing I've done," he told *Friday* magazine.

He's not kidding. The two Avengers films have so far grossed over $3 billion dollars. Audiences around the world flocked to see Captain America join forces with other heroes like Iron Man, The Hulk, and Thor.

Captain America and the other superheroes team up to save the world in *The Avengers*.

Chris took his prep for the role very seriously. He spent months following a strict weight training **regimen** to bulk up for the role. Chris even took gymnastics classes and did special exercises designed to boost his power and speed.

regimen—a dedicated routine

Fast Fact

Chris wasn't into comic books as a kid, so he had to study for the Captain America role. He kept a copy of *Mythos: Captain America* by his side during filming for inspiration. This Marvel comic book tells the origin story of Captain America.

Chapter 5

Behind the Scenes

On the outside many actors appear confident and cool. But for Chris that's often not the case. He often feels nervous at auditions, interviews, and on high-pressure movie sets. "I struggle with **anxiety** sometimes, especially when promoting films," Chris told *Shortlist* magazine.

Staying Zen

One of the things that helps Chris handle the stress is Buddhism. Often thought of as a religion, Buddhism is actually an ancient philosophy about finding **enlightenment**. Chris has practiced Buddhism since age 17. His beliefs keep him calm amid the hectic world of Hollywood.

"I love acting. It's my playground, it lets me explore," he has said. "But my happiness in this world, my level of peace, is never going to be dictated by acting."

anxiety—a feeling of worry or nervousness

enlightenment—a state of understanding and wisdom

Chris enjoyed attending the 2015 Academy Awards.

Fast Fact

A former professional dancer, Chris' mom has a tap dancing floor in her house's basement. Chris often tap dances there to blow off steam!

A World of Good

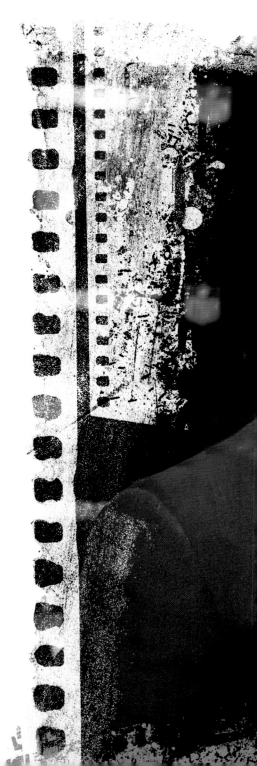

It's inspiring when superheroes use their powers for good. Chris Evans does just that off-screen. In fact, he thinks kids battling illness are the "true superheroes." That's why he often does charity work at children's hospitals.

In 2015 Chris teamed up with actor Chris Pratt to raise money to help sick kids. Together they raised almost $27,000 for Seattle Children's Hospital and Christopher's Haven. The two action stars made a Twitter bet on the Super Bowl XLIX game between the Seattle Seahawks and the New England Patriots. Whoever lost the bet would have to visit the other's hometown hospital in costume. Chris's beloved Patriots took the victory. But being the hero he is, he dressed up as Captain America anyway to surprise the kids at Seattle Children's Hospital. Pratt returned the favor, visiting Christopher's Haven as his character Star-Lord from the film *Guardians of the Galaxy*.

Chris has also used his star status to spotlight Got Your 6, an organization that helps military veterans. Alhough he may play tough characters in the movies, this actor is all heart.

"[To me], heroism is putting yourself last ... putting other people's needs before your own."

–Chris on being a hero

Chris appeared with actor Chris Pratt (right) at the National Football League Honors in 2015.

A New Direction

Like any good action hero, Chris continues to move full steam ahead! Captain America made another appearance in 2016 in *Captain America: Civil War*. But aside from his acting work, Chris has expressed strong interest in working behind the camera. He's already had a great start with *Before We Go*, released in 2014. Chris did double-duty on this romantic comedy, both starring in and directing the film. Audiences embraced his efforts. The movie brought in $1.53 million in video sales before it ever hit the theaters.

It's clear that whatever Chris Evans takes on, he gives it his all. And his legions of fans can't wait to see what his future efforts bring.

"Sometimes you can invest a lot in a movie and have a great experience yourself, but for it also to be well-received is a real treat."

—Chris on the rewards of being an action movie star

Chris was chosen as Favorite Action Movie Actor in the 2015 People's Choice Awards.

GLOSSARY

anxiety (ang-ZAHY-i-tee)—a feeling of worry or nervousness

aspiring (uh-SPY-uh-ring)—having a goal to do something specific

black box theater (blak boks THEE-uh-ter)—a simple theater, usually with black walls, that can be adapted to any kind of performance

cosmic (KOZ-mik)—having to do with the universe and the stars

enlightenment (en-LAHYT-en-muhnt)—a state of understanding and wisdom

formulaic (for-myuh-LEY-ik)—following a predictable pattern

heist (hahyst)—a robbery

improvised (IM-pruh-vahyzd)—made up on the spot

internship (IN-turn-ship)—a temporary job in which a person works with and learns from experienced workers

pilot (PY-lut)—a test to see how a TV series performs with an audience before it is bought by a network

recurring (ri-KUR-ing)—happening over and over again

regimen (REJ-uh-men)—a dedicated routine

sequel (SEE-kwul)—a story that continues an existing story, taking it forward in time

telekinesis (tel-i-ki-NEE-sis)—the ability to move something by thought or will power, without using physical force

READ MORE

Garza, Sarah. *Action! Making Movies.* Time for Kids Nonfiction Readers. Huntington Beach, Calif.: Teacher Created Materials, 2013.

Misiroglu, Gina. *The Superhero Book: The Ultimate Encyclopedia of Comic-Book Icons and Hollywood Heroes.* Canton, Mich.: Visible Ink Press, 2012.

Quijano, Jonathan. *Make Your Own Action Thriller.* Make Your Movie. North Mankato, Minn.: Capstone Press, 2012.

INTERNET SITES

FactHound offers a safe, fun way to find Internet sites related to this book. All of the sites on FactHound have been researched by our staff.

Here's all you do:

Visit *www.facthound.com*

Type in this code: 9781515712381

 **Super-cool stuff!** Check out projects, games and lots more at **www.capstonekids.com**

INDEX